Tipton

Tipton Poetry Journal, located in Indiana, publishes quality poetry from Indiana and around the world.

This issue features 41 poets from the United States (20 different states) and 3 poets from Canada, India, and the Phillipines.

Our Featured Poem this issue is "Nocturnal" written by Sara Sarna. Sara's poem, which also receives an award of $25, can be found on page 9. The featured poem was chosen by the Board of Directors of Brick Street Poetry, Inc., the Indiana non-profit organization who publishes *Tipton Poetry Journal*.

Dan Carpenter reviews Linda Neal Reising's *The Keeping*.

Cover Photo: "Snowman 2021" by Barry Harris.

Print versions of *Tipton Poetry Journal* are available for purchase through <u>amazon.com</u>.

Barry Harris, Editor

Copyright 2021 by the Tipton Poetry Journal.

All rights remain the exclusive property of the individual contributors and may not be used without their permission.

Tipton Poetry Journal is published by Brick Street Poetry Inc., a tax-exempt non-profit organization under IRS Code 501(c)(3). Brick Street Poetry Inc. publishes the Tipton Poetry Journal, hosts the monthly poetry series *Poetry on Brick Street* and sponsors other poetry-related events.

Contents

G Timothy Gordon 1

Jennifer Ruth Jackson 2

Robert S. King 4

Simona Carini 6

Shakiba Hashemi 7

Jack e Lorts 8

Sara Sarna 9

Seth Rosenbloom 10

Tobi Alfier 11

Michael Salcman 12

Charlene Langfur 14

Julie L. Moore 15

Diane Glancy 18

Raj Sharma 19

Charles Grosel 20

Ken Meisel 21

Lynn Pattison 24

Timothy Robbins 25

Nancy Kay Peterson 26

Bruce Levine 27

George Moore 28

Thomas Osatchoff 30

Dave Seter 31

James Eric Watkins 32

Michael E. Strosahl 33

Mary Shanley 34

Michele Penn Diaz 35

Matthew Brennan	36
Jerry Jerome	37
J. Lintu	38
James Croal Jackson	40
Cameron Morse	41
Diane Webster	42
C.T. Holte	44
Theresa Monteiro	45
Michael Jones	46
Alan Cohen	46
Jonathan Bracker	48
Hamilton Salsich	49
Akshaya Pawaskar	50
Karla Linn Merrifield	52
Leslie Schultz	53
Ken Craft	54
Mary Hills Kuck	55
Review: The Keeping by Linda Neal Reising	**56**
Contributor Biographies	61

Becoming Us
G Timothy Gordon

> We are returned to what lay beneath the beauty. — Jack Gilbert

Storms raging elsewhere out there,
country, culture, old order unhinged,
pitch-black fires not lit by dead-summer
Sonoran heat, dawn-stoked 110°, & climbing,
like blunt June blue moon, while we hunker-down
for years, it seems, *One World Together at Home*,
yearning for human heat & grand passion,
full flowering life we thought we knew,
willing to settle, fast-track color and fall
into bitter winter, countless, moonless nights
swiping the iPhone, bingeing the tube,
home fires blazing.

G Timothy Gordon lives in Las Cruces, New Mexico. His eighth book, *Dream Wind,* was published December 2019 (Spirit-of-the-Ram Press). Work appears in *AGNI, American Literary Review, Cincinnati Review, Kansas Quarterly, Louisville Review, Mississippi Review, New York Quarterly, Phoebe, RHINO, Sonora Review, Texas Observer*, among others. *Everything Speaking Chinese* received Riverstone Books' Poetry Book Prize. Recognitions include NEA & NEH Fellowships, residencies, and several Pushcart nominations. His chapbook, *Empty Heaven, Empty Earth,* will be published Spring-Summer 2021. He divides professional & personal lives among Asia, the Southwest, & Maine.

Winter Light
Jennifer Ruth Jackson

Aurora borealis zigzags
Crease night's obsidian veil
Stars stand apart
White-faced pallbearers

Shifting greens float like a
Dancer's dress baring
Legs, granting peeks at
Heaven's skin

Tearing grief and wonder
From moon's watchful
Eye in frozen multicolor
Faith

Astronomy in Time
Jennifer Ruth Jackson

We constructed a new moon
with half-empty wine bottles
and half-dead stars. Gazers,
we rested our backs on a hill
darker than the sky in its navy
blazer. You were my Copernicus
and I, your Galileo—all bright
theories and significance.
We cut slices of the universe
and fed each other, grasping
cosmos and hands decades apart.

2020 Changes

Jennifer Ruth Jackson

We bump elbows
upon meeting...
gloved hands
near our chests.
We disagree on
basic definitions.
"Distance" is
the number of feet
in a checkout line.
"Pandemic triage"
morphs into "medically-
condoned eugenics".
"Essential" gains
six meanings, not
all necessary.
Everything tastes
of faint chlorine...
even your lover's
tongue.

Jennifer Ruth Jackson is an award-winning poet and fiction writer living in Wisconsin whose work has appeared in *Red Earth Review, Banshee*, and more. She runs a blog for disabled and neurodivergent creatives called *The Handy, Uncapped Pen* from an apartment she shares with her husband. Follow her on Twitter @jenruthjackson.

Social Distancing
Robert S. King

Much more than six feet away,
a neighbor cleans his gutters.
At a safe distance, another watches
through the face shield of her window.

I dare outside toward the empty street
to fetch spam mail and bills from my box,
leaving my housebound computer wheezing
as it tries to disinfect a virus.

Even electronics get infected,
but today the gutterman's faith
tests positive as he whistles
while he works.

Across this vast space,
the man on wobbling ladder
spots my courageous voyage
and tears off his mask
so that from a distant world
he can at least yell hello.

Rising Wind

Robert S. King

— In memoriam, poet Joan Colby, 2020

Wind takes your last breath
higher than the weight of the world,
lifts your voice that we still hear
flowing around the earth.
You will sing to us forever
who sing along
in every breath we take.

Robert S. King lives in Athens, Georgia, where he serves on the board of FutureCycle Press and edits *Good Works Review*. His poems have appeared in hundreds of magazines, including *Atlanta Review, California Quarterly, Chariton Review, Hollins Critic, Kenyon Review, Main Street Rag, Midwest Quarterly, Negative Capability, Southern Poetry Review, and Spoon River Poetry Review*. He has published eight poetry collections, most recently *Diary of the Last Person on Earth* (Sybaritic Press 2014), *Developing a Photograph of God* (Glass Lyre Press, 2014), and *Messages from Multiverses* (Duck Lake Books, 2020). His personal website is www.robertsking.info.

The Body's Refusal to Function as Intended
Simona Carini

I take a bite from an apple, make a hollow,
chew slowly, halt: cannot swallow.

When muscles work in concert, in sequence, actions follow.
Not now, though: nothing moves and I cannot swallow.

With effort I shove the bolus down, stow the apple.
Inhaling hurts: I'm lacerated inside by the hard swallow.

I reel and through closed eyes I probe the sorrow:
What is it my body refuses to swallow?

Friends want my help when lovers leave them hollow,
teachers press me towards a choice they want me to swallow.

My parents' grieving silence grinds me: I should live at home
until I marry, work close by—customs I refuse to swallow.

If I cannot feed myself, I'll waste away, turn hollow.
Enough of demands and complaints. I'll fly away as my own swallow.

Born in Perugia, Italy, a graduate of the Catholic University of the Sacred Heart (Milan, Italy) and of Mills College (Oakland, California), **Simona Carini** writes poetry and nonfiction and has been published in various venues, in print and online, including *Intima - A Journal of Narrative Medicine, Italian Americana, Sheila-Na-Gig Online*, the *Journal of Humanistic Mathematics*, the *American Journal of Nursing, Star 82 Review*. She lives in Northern California with her husband and works as a data scientist at an academic research institution. Her website is https://simonacarini.com

Shade of the Clock
Shakiba Hashemi

When you recognize that there is a voice in your head that pretends to be you and never stops speaking, you are awakening out of your unconscious identification with the stream of thinking.
— Eckhart Tolle

Inspired by the book "Power of Now" by Eckhart Tolle

I barricade myself in the dark.
I see a reflection of myself
in the bathroom mirror, covered with heavy steam
of the running hot water. *I can't be found.*
I dye my jet-black hair blonde and put on a red lipstick.
I frantically search for something
to mask my distinct tattoo. I wrap my left bicep
in gauze, but still see the green scorpion's tail
peeking out of my mummified arm. I jump
when I hear the rattle of the old pipes in the motel room,
rusting more with each clunk. *I can't be found.*
An uneasy feeling flashes through my flesh,
a swarm of ants are struggling to escape
from my clogged brain. I pierce my eyelids
and my tongue, to open the pores for them
to crawl out from within. My droopy shoulders
drop my weight onto my knees, and they give in.
I can't live with myself any longer.
The words echo in my head with a vibrating shock.
The echo keeps getting louder,
I can't live with myself any longer.
How many of me are there? Can they both talk?
Which is the unlucky one my high school friends used to mock?
If one is found, the other can still be.
Maybe the survivor is the real me.
I must hold on for one more day.
The air is so crisp I'm afraid to crack it, so I don't move.
I'm still conscious, lying on the floor,
watching the ticking shade of the clock.

Shakiba Hashemi is an Iranian-American poet, painter and teacher living in Southern California. She is a bilingual poet, and writes in English and Farsi. She holds a BFA in Drawing and Painting from Laguna College of Art and Design. Her work has recently appeared in *Atlanta Review* and is forthcoming in *I-70 Review* and the New York Quarterly Anthology *Without a Doubt: poems illuminating faith.*

January 6, 2021

Jack e Lorts

It was the usual day of joy
in the Columbia River Gorge
along the River of Life.
What was taking place elsewhere,
we didn't know.
We didn't know America was
falling into an abyss,
that walls were crumbling,
little men climbing into darkness,
into an abyss.

It was the usual day of joy
in the Columbia River Gorge
along the River of Life.
What was befalling others elsewhere,
we didn't know,
what was changing light into darkness,
sweetness into the bitterest gall,
Icarus falling slowly from the sky.

It was the usual day of joy
along the River of Life.

A retired educator living in a small town in eastern Oregon, **Jack e Lorts** has appeared widely, if infrequently, over the past 50+ years such places as *Arizona Quarterly, Kansas Quarterly, English Journal, Chiron Review, Tipton Poetry Journal, verse daily* among others. Author of three previous chapbooks, his *The Love Songs of Epram Pratt* appeared in 2019 from Uttered Chaos Press.

Nocturnal

Sara Sarna

There's a coyote in the field.
He has the look I wear
when I'm not sure why
I find myself where I am,
though his may have
more to do with uncertainty
about the daylight.
The raccoon family crossing the road
has that same bemused look,
babies stopping in the middle,
unsure of the sun
and whether, at that moment,
their parents can be trusted.
I, never nocturnal, wake
as the sun merely considers rising,
sleep as much a mystery as God.
We are, as a whole, confused
by a world no longer familiar,
a construct of time
that no longer applies,
and we wait for our eyes to adjust.

Sara Sarna is a poet in southeastern Wisconsin. She is a military "brat" and only put down roots as an adult. Her work has appeared in print, online and on stage. Her first chapbook, *Whispers from a Bench*, was published in November of 2020.

Empty

Seth Rosenbloom

A place on the counter
the piles of the papers
that you left, that I moved

That you hated me for moving
that I thought I was right to move
right for moving

That I thought were left
behind, left to go elsewhere
left to go where they belong

Because I always do the moving
because I moved them
because I thought I was right

Empty, that place on the kitchen counter
bracketed by the keys to the Honda
and a coffee mug

Sun streaking across the granite
to a place on the counter
to a place that is now empty

And it catches me
in its emptiness
for what is now not there

The piles that I moved
to make space
because I wanted the space

But I did not want to be empty

Seth Rosenbloom grew up outside Washington D.C. and lives in Seattle. He studied acting at Boston University and received a BA in Drama from the University of Washington. Alongside a career in management consulting, he has written and acted in solo performances at On the Boards, Bumbershoot and on the Seattle Channel. He studies poetry at Hugo House, and is working on a collection of poems about coming of age and loss.

Two Hours by Train
Tobi Alfier

Last evening the rain was soft as a child's footsteps
sneaking down stairs to a heated front room.
And on this late morning, out the lace-curtained window,
on the mountain two hours away by train—
a thick cover of snow, rarely seen by anyone in any season.

Mama and Junior turned the couch around
so we could watch this lovely lady in her satin gown.
How the light shimmered past the tree line.
We knew this could not be embraced or kept
except in memories. I ran and got my notebook

full of notes on all the sorrows and sadnesses
of this failing town—dayworkers and old families
stuck along the riverfront with nowhere to run.
It was an honor to sketch the beauty of this view,
a magnolia blossom in the dark hair of the mountain.

Mama made us pancakes. And hot chocolate.
We ate right there, our eyes glued to the sight.
Tonight we'll light one candle, give thanks.
For once I was a grateful daughter. I knew
that never again would I get this story right.

Tobi Alfier is a multiple Pushcart nominee and multiple Best of the Net nominee. *Slices of Alice & Other Character Studies* was published by Cholla Needles Press. *Symmetry: earth and sky* was published by Main Street Rag. She is co-editor of *San Pedro River Review*(www.bluehorsepress.com) and lives in California.

The Coup
Michael Salcman

When the generals come they will be dressed in suits and ties.
They will bear titles
like delegate and representative of the people.
They will feed the widow
and bury the child.
Each spring the garden will grow the same apple
passing it from tree to tree.
The catamount will sing with the strongest,
the worker in his mirror, the police in their cars.
My tulip poplars will lose their blossoms at the start of Spring.

The generals will make peace with our enemies
and war with our friends.
They will make gods of themselves
and slaves of their subjects.
They will smile in the afternoon
and frown at midnight.
They will pass laws for others but not for themselves.
They will still look like the sort of Boy Scout
who helps an old lady cross a street against her will.

They always tell us attendance is voluntary
but don't fail to come to the meetings.

Gratitude

Michael Salcman

Thank God for science, for the two eyes,
Two hands and two ears
That investigate the world
For the brain that invents its own world
For the feet that know when to turn away
For the heart that knows when to pray
For the nose that goes just ahead of us
And the generations who went before
For the gift of DNA, in all its stability
And mutability
For the love of charm and spore
Invisible neutrino and weighty quark
The animals who left the ark
And that blessed wedge between light and dark.

Michael Salcman: poet, physician and art historian, was chairman of neurosurgery at the University of Maryland and president of the Contemporary Museum. Poems appear in *Arts & Letters, The Café Review, Hopkins Review, The Hudson Review, New Letters,* and *Poet Lore.* Books include *The Clock Made of Confetti, The Enemy of Good is Better, Poetry in Medicine,* his popular anthology of classic and contemporary poems on doctors, patients, illness & healing, *A Prague Spring, Before & After,* winner of the 2015 Sinclair Poetry Prize, and *Shades & Graces,* inaugural winner of The Daniel Hoffman Legacy Book Prize (Spuyten Duyvil, 2020). He lives in Baltimore.

Practicing Peace

Charlene Langfur

Each day I think connecting with spirit matters,
especially now in the world of the pandemic
when loss and illness is everywhere around.
I sit quietly to start this practice off for me,
wish others well, breathe deep, breathe in and out
and start over, counting breaths, a woman like myself
living in the big heat of the Sonoran desert next
to the fan palms and yucca and the century plants and
the old oasis palms where the crows sit on the tree top to rest.
I am doing the same, taking to the oasis in the middle
of the day, bowing my head quietly as if it will avail
kindness and compassion, stopping to smile at my
13-pound honey colored dog upside down on the couch,
enthralled with time and space itself, balanced, at ease.
Last night the pink roses on the kitchen table
opened up so wide they fell over the edges of the glass,
as if open armed, one petal above another and another.
I know this is how it is now for many of us, opening up
like a flower, practicing the same, one bud at a time

Charlene Langfur lives in Palm Springs, California, and is a southern Californian, an organic gardener, a Syracuse University Graduate Writing Fellow. Her most recent publications include poems in *Emrys, Inlandia, North Dakota Quarterly*, and a series of poems forthcoming in *Weber – The Contemporary West*.

Working Backwards
Julie L. Moore

When I confront a human being as my Thou and speak the basic word I-Thou to him, then he is no thing among things nor does he consist of things. . . . [H]e is Thou and fills the firmament. Not as if there were nothing but he; but everything else lives in his light. ~Martin Buber

I thread through the Society of Friends' Historic

Estates of Serenity, the avenue winding

between both sides of the cemetery
hosting turkey vultures that loiter

close to an opossum run over last night.
The scene reminds me of Fibonacci
and his numbers, each one the sum

of the previous two: 1, 1, 2, 3,
5, 8, 13, and so on, ad infinitum.
So here I am, one driver meandering
through, as a second comes the other
way, the animal between us, in the center

of the street, and suddenly, we are three.
The five buzzards swoop in,
their primordial urges limited to the turn
each takes, beaks like pliers
riving flesh from bone, reddening the road,
and we are eight. I can write that now
as 8 because of Fibonacci, whose *Liber Abaci*
converted Europe to Hindu-Arabic numerals,

abandoning the smooth stones of the abacus.
More magical than he knew, his numbers
conjured the spirits of Euclid and Pythagoras
through division, making all answers golden:
mean, cut, ratio. Did I mention I'm on my way
to church this Sunday morning? And that the Greeks
weren't right about everything? Symmetry
isn't necessary for beauty, no, I need only
the slow-order railroad to my left
and the swift Mississinewa River to my right,
striking a curious balance between sensation
and relation, *It* and *Thou*, perimeter
of the burial ground, that center of gravity.

The sum total of everything I am
drives me to worship where I join
sisters and brothers—all of us from so many broken
backgrounds, we don't keep count—
where we know we're black and brown and white
and more than numbers, the architecture
of our body asymmetrical—not uniform
but unified, buttressed

by our faith in the Lord our God,
who we pray will integrate this hour,
exorcise the spirit of the lynching
not so long ago from this city:
the three taken to the tree—

O, how the vultures circled then—
the two bludgeoned and strung up—
unwilling icons in the photo

sold by the thousands—and the one
let go, returned to his cell.

I forgive them, he said, words heavy with light,

a backwards kind of work, filling the firmament.

Augury
Julie L. Moore

He stands by the stop light, where the off-
ramp from Route 69 meets West McGalliard.
And every time I arrive, I'm empty-

handed, with no food or drink to offer,
coins clattering in the console like useless beliefs.
BP's the only place within miles. To get to this point,

perhaps he hitchhikes or walks along paths with no
sidewalks, no houses, nothing but scorching grass
and iron weed, the chicory closing up shop

when the sun unbridles its white-hot bronco.
An island of wrappers and water bottles,
some drained, some still full, lies behind him.

We wait while the signal's red beam begins

to consume us. As a horse-fly blunders
onto my windshield, Saint Matthew

mumbles in my mind about *the least of these*
and the radio's song proclaims, *This is it,
the apocalypse*. The mendicant talks incessantly, to no

one in particular, so loudly, I can hear him
through my unopened window. Saliva and sweat
saturate his bushy beard. He lifts his tattered sign

that names his need but doesn't really beg, just faces
the Silverado ahead of me, its steel ashen from wear.
He who hesitates is lost, my father would say

when I was a kid, urging me to *choose*,
choose, even in this age when nothing
is certain, when my money might feed

a habit, when we have the poor with us always,
no matter what I do. I long
to help him anyway—what burden

is he to me?—but maybe I'm actually
tired of trafficking in guilt. The light turns.
Clouds to the west grow mad.

I have to go, have to pass by him while he wipes
his brow with the sleeve of his dingy shirt,
then eyes the next cars coming towards him.

Julie L. Moore is the author of four poetry collections, including, most recently, *Full Worm Moon*, which won a 2018 Woodrow Hall Top Shelf Award and received honorable mention for the Conference on Christianity and Literature's 2018 Book of the Year. A Best of the Net and five-time Pushcart Prize nominee, she has also published poetry in *Alaska Quarterly Review, African American Review, Image, New Ohio Review, Poetry Daily, Prairie Schooner, The Southern Review,* and *Verse Daily*.  Her work likewise has appeared in several anthologies, including *Becoming: What Makes a Woman*, published by University of Nebraska Gender Programs, and *Every River On Earth: Writing from Appalachian Ohio*, published by Ohio University Press. Moore is an Associate Professor of English and the Writing Center Director at Taylor University, where she is the poetry editor of *Relief Journal*. You can learn more about her work at julielmoore.com.

Reck-loose [my] Re-cluse
Diane Glancy

I saw a crow in a dress. In contemplation of
flame— of fire— of encroaching blaze.

I will give you what you desire— [Merton]. Your
solitude will be armed against you. You will be left
alone. In your own place. The flames will pass over
you. You will be earless. Noseless. The
protrusions go first. You will be without trappings
that cannot be done without. Your fingers will be
gone though you raise your arms to spare them.
Your toes will not last. You will walk on ankles.
Your clerical collar ashed. Your long skirts.

They gather silver, and brass, and iron, and lead,
and tin, in the midst of the furnace, to blow the fire
upon it, to melt it— Ezekiel 22:20. The searing less
gripping now as you become used to the cautery.

You know outside the flames it is cold.

Diane Glancy is professor emerita at Macalester College. Currently, she teaches in the low-residency MFA program at Carlow University in Pittsburgh. Her latest poetry book, *Island of the Innocent, a Consideration of the Book of Job*, was published by Turtle Point Press in 2020. *A Line of Driftwood, a story of Ada Blackjack* is forthcoming from Turtle Point in 2021. Broadleaf Press will publish a collection of nonfiction in 2021, *Still Moving, How the Road, the Land and the Sacred Shape a Life*. Her awards and other books are on her website www.dianeglancy.com

A Morning at Milwaukee

Raj Sharma

Sipping coffee, I look out
my lakeside cottage window

at the Michigan, its cobalt blue
flaring suddenly to the gold

of a new day, while the geese
go gliding away

to test new waters. A morning
like this calls for opening ourselves

to the real import of
the quotidian events of the day.

Like watching the landlady
across the lawns in her kitchen

as she taps her feet to the galloping rhythm
of Beethoven's *"Rage over a Lost Penny"*.

All she does is to cook
an everyday breakfast,

yet she flavours it with her elan,
and her deep caring

for those she loves.
Thus might each morning

of mine begin, by pouring all
my love into the meanest

tasks. Thus might I light up
the drab, common day.

Raj Sharma lives in North Carolina and is a retired senior professor of English who has worked at universities in India, Middle East and USA. Published work includes two collections of short stories, *A Strange Wind Blowing* (2019) and *In My Arms* (2000) and a collection of poems, *No Season for Grief* (2017). Over forty poems and short stories have appeared in magazines like *Grey Sparrow, North Dakota Quarterly, Crossways, The American Aesthetic, SNReview. South Jersey Underground, The Monarch Review, Folly, JD Review, The Fine Line, TWJ Magazine, The Missing Slate, Exercise Bowler, Rock and Sling, Ascent Aspirations, Dr TJ Eckleburg Review, New Mercury Magazine* and others.

Time
Charles Grosel

Time is not a pencil sharpened to
extinction, a ballpoint run out of ink.
Time does not count off the mile markers
nor is it the oscilloscope's blip that
disappears at the orb's right hand then
returns at the left to start again. Time
does not press its truths in layers for
later excavation, jealous of its dead.
Time is not a formula or equation,
not an algorithm, not the theory
or the experiment that tests it. It's
more the tinkling of a music box in a
movie by Renoir, a pinwheel spinning,
everything at once and nothing at all.

Our Lump of Clay
Charles Grosel

What bulwark faith in the face of death?
Does it matter when matter flees us?
Does it ease pain? Fear? The looming black
hole of a life at end, our span but
the twitch of a rabbit in the bush,
a bird. For all this talk of Spirit,
we do so cling to our lump of clay.

An editor, writer, and poet, **Charles Grosel** grew up in the suburbs of Cleveland, Ohio. After stints on both the West and East Coasts, he now lives in Arizona with his wife and daughter. He studied English literature at Yale University and fiction writing at the University of California at Davis, where he was a Regent's Fellow. To earn a living, he has been a teacher, editor, trainer, and ghost writer, among other jobs, but through it all he has kept at his true vocation, writing poetry and fiction. He has published stories in journals such as *Western Humanities Review, Fiction Southeast, Water-Stone,* and *The MacGuffin,* as well as poems in *Slate, The Threepenny Review, Poet Lore, Cream City Review,* and *Harpur Palate*. Charles owns the communications firm, Write for Success (write4success.net). *The Sound of Rain Without Water,* a chapbook of poems, came out in December 2020.

The Angel of Doo Wop
Ken Meisel

snaked up to me in a dive bar
somewhere down south,
and it placed my finger over the knob
that punched *I Only Have Eyes for You* –
by the Flamingos – so that I could hear
the echo of harmonic voices
lifting up and humming in the stars
over a swamp behind us,
and a lonesome woman, a blond,
gazed over into my eyes –
she was probably sensing
something real, some signal
from the heart
she felt, or remembered,
as millions of people go by
but, gazing into me, they all
disappeared from view
because, her eyes said to me,
I only have eyes for you.
And I leaned across the wooden bar;
I gazed back into her
earth angel eyes as if
telling her she would be
the only one I adore.
Then the Five Satins, *In the Still
Of the Night*, played –
a man in a Levis jacket
had shuffled over and pressed it to play –
and the echoes
of the glassware tinkling in the bar
pulsed like stars, like eyes
watching over us: over
our sad beauty, over our
inescapable matter,
over our nights in May when we
claim our love for one
another and, in the still
of the night, a man outdoors –
(we could see him through
the glazed bar window –)
stood rocking on the step

of an empty building
playing his exquisite saxophone
to that part of Being he,
himself,
could never play to –
except by and through
the sublime strobe lights of God
flooding his horn
with all the incandescent light
that the stars and fate
are made of,
and the sad doo wop angel
leaned over to me,
drink in hand, and said,
you know Kant was correct
when he mumbled
beauty is the only finality here,
and the song on the juke box
was *Come Softly to Me* by the Fleetwoods,
and the girl's voices,
silken across the mic,
thrilled me
until I was a mirror
somersaulting me back
to my own desire;
to the love songs
of winsome school girls
with scarlet ribbons;
and the angel pointed me
toward the infinite veils
of beauty that, in this bar,
because they are
from the other mansion
on the hill – and I mean
that house we can't see
but only feel with the
the heart's espionage of poetry –
because of this
they are absolutely
without equivocation,
without reflection,
without hesitation
born from that light
most glad of all,
and, because of that,

because they baptize
and caress
our tender spirits
with an exquisite magic
that comforts our sadness
and our gladness
until we're no longer
sore,
because of this
they're everlasting –
forever
and for always,
amen.

Ken Meisel is a poet and psychotherapist, a 2012 Kresge Arts Literary Fellow, a Pushcart Prize nominee and the author of eight books of poetry. His most recent books are: *Our Common Souls: New & Selected Poems of Detroit* (Blue Horse Press: 2020) and *Mortal Lullabies* (FutureCycle Press: 2018). Meisel has recent work in *Concho River Review, I-70 Review, San Pedro River Review,* and *Rabid Oak*. Ken lives in Dearborn, Michigan.

I helped him bury the goat
Lynn Pattison

that last autumn we were together.
Understand, he'd had that goat a long time
there on his faded farm, and he didn't say much

as we dragged the carcass toward
the pasture. I see his slim figure in sunlight
by the rusting fence. It was hot. I was not used

to grave-digging. The hole needed
to be bigger than I'd imagined. What was
I doing there, in love with a penniless farmer,

sweating and huffing to deepen
a grave? The barnyard animals,
silent at first, grew uneasy. Stiff-legged,

the cow bolted toward me then froze.
A goat smashed headlong into barn siding.
I tucked into the work, unnerved, that close to death.

When it was done we cleaned up,
walked behind the slumped barn to pick
the last of the pears. I climbed the tree to hand

them down. But they were too soft.
Gone to mush. You can't let them ripen
on the tree, he said, they break down at the core.

[This poem first appeared online at Atticus Press in 2013.]

Lynn Pattison lives in Kalamazoo, Michigan. Her work has appeared in *Ruminate, Moon City Review, The Mom Egg Review, Glassworks Magazine* and *Notre Dame Review*, among others, and has been anthologized widely. Her published collections include the book, *Light That Sounds Like Breaking* (Mayapple Press), and three chapbooks: *tesla's daughter* (March St. Press), *Walking Back the Cat* (Bright Hill Press), and *Matryoshka Houses*, released last summer from Kelsay Press. Her book mss, *Milky Way Stardust Aquarium* is in search of a loving home.

Aldi Left and Right
Timothy Robbins

On the left as you enter, in buckets
aimed like cannons, the usual
bouquets of down-on-their-luck
Voltaires. On the right, a woman
pumps clear hand-sanitizer into
one palm and rubs it in with the
lotion motions her husband

watches (and sometimes sees)
every night before she gathers
herself next to him (sometimes
close) under the sheets. It's not
that shoppers usually swap looks.
It's that they notice the lack
now that some follow CDC guide-

lines their neighbors trespass.
You sing into your mask. You
feel the good cheer gather there
floating in a pocket of carbon
dioxide. Are any other shoppers
leaking songs? None you can hear.
Some may stick our their tongues.

Timothy Robbins has been teaching English as a Second Language for 30 years. His poems have appeared in many literary journals and has published five volumes of poetry: *Three New Poets* (Hanging Loose Press), *Denny's Arbor Vitae* (Adelaide Books), *Carrying Bodies* (Main Street Rag Press) *Mother Wheel* (Cholla Needles Press) and *This Night I Sup in Your House* (Cyberwit.net). He lives in Wisconsin with his husband of 22 years.

Plains Pioneer

Nancy Kay Peterson

I swim against the blizzard,
one arm sweeping drifts down to mid-thigh height,
one hand grasping the icy rope
that leads from cabin to barn.
It has snowed for days.

This trip had to be made.
A blast of super cold wind
takes my breath away.
I stumble, lose my balance,
my hold on the rope.

I grope frantically, eyes tearing,
Nothing. I know I should not crawl
blindly, but I am floundering.
My fingers numbing, will no longer
recognize the feel of a lifeline.

Anything is better than not trying to survive.
I stagger for hours, for days, for years.
I think I must be close.
Warmed by my efforts, I pause
to enjoy the balmy breeze, perfect for sleeping.

The snow is no longer falling.
Everything is angelic white.
You don't freeze to death quickly.
The sun rises in the east
A bloody ball.

Nancy Kay Peterson's poetry has appeared in print and online in numerous publications, including most *recently Lost Lake Folk Opera, One Sentence Poems, Spank the Carp* and *Three Line Poetry*. From 2004-2009, she was co-publisher and co-editor of *Main Channel Voices: A Dam Fine Literary Magazine*. Her chapbook, *Belated Remembrance*, was published by Finishing Line Press in 2010. A second chapbook, *Selling the Family*, is due out soon. She lives in Winona, Minnesota.

Diminished Light
Bruce Levine

Diminished light
As the day moves toward evening
Shadows begin to form
The sun drifts below the horizon
Evening shadows spreading gently
And the sky changing from blue to gray
Awaiting the stars to appear
Amid the ghost of the moon
Forecasting the blackening of the sky
The yellow sun gone
Replaced from west to east
As the white orb ascends
The moon casting a new light
Pulling the tides as it pulls the day
From light to dark
In a never-ending pattern of the solar system
Amid the vastness of the Universe

Bruce Levine, a 2019 Pushcart Prize Poetry Nominee, has spent his life as a writer of fiction and poetry and as a music and theatre professional. Over 300 of his works are published in over 25 on-line journals including *Ariel Chart, Friday Flash Fiction, Literary Yard;* over 30 print books including *Poetry Quarterly, Haiku Journal, Dual Coast Magazine*, and his shows have been produced in New York and around the country. Six eBooks are available from Amazon.com. His work is dedicated to the loving memory of his late wife, Lydia Franklin. He lives in New York with his dog, Daisy. Visit him at www.brucelevine.com.

The Island
George Moore

The sea is scratched glass
and in turn it scratches glass and knees

the sea some monstrous beginning
always beginning again and I am

not use to it this deep
wood at its edge like an ingrown wall of trees

I am more the mountain ruach
calling from an outcropping above timberline

seeing all the way across a day's walk west
and feeling empty in an airless home

But the islands are out there
just beyond this rumbling edge

An old Orthodox woman all in black
sits on a garden wall

and pulls the skin from a rabbit in a single jerk
and holds it up an offering

to her unknown god or the space she fills
But mine are the gods of infinite surmise

the echoes off crowns of snowy peaks
the emptiness of canyons crying back

I am never an island or the sea surrounding it
where the fishermen go out

in their damaged boats on glass
and the winds deny them peace

and they haul their traps in nightly dreams
and they live through that another season

No I am the island that is unseen
a foot in the sand one on a foreign peak

I am the rabbit a single moment before
the gods tell us to wait

George Moore's poetry has appeared in *The Atlantic, North American Review, Colorado Review, Orion, Arc, Tipton Poetry Journal* and *Stand*. His most recent collections are *Children's Drawings of the Universe* (Salmon Poetry 2015) and *Saint Agnes Outside the Walls* (FururecCycle 2016). He is a seven-time Pushcart Prize nominee, and finalist for The National Poetry Series. His work was recently shortlisted for the Bailieborough Poetry Prize and long-listed for both the Gregory O'Donoghue and Ginkgo Poetry Prizes. Retired from the University of Colorado, Boulder, he lives on the south shore of Nova Scotia.

Leaning into this Frontier to Find a Cure Before We Get Hit Again
Thomas Osatchoff

by actual meteors or the redirected light of our ideas of meteors
driving in the wind of themselves
the size of small cars
on mile long shifting selfdoms of withering iron words
cracking spectrums in nickel silicate pieces of themselves
eyeing eyes what they hit like

the dry climate, obligated, says:
still have to edit the whole thing.
Flat mesa tops separated by steep canyons
blanketed equally by the striving of the night, blue day.
Flash-floods raging change on the innumerable caravan
along the mind of the arroyo wanting to feed its family.

Location chosen for its relative inaccessibility.
What is the name of the location? Punctuated—

the land feels

by way of animals showing us the way. Here are some hints:
black bears (brown-color variation), elk, mule deer, gray foxes,
bobcats, skunks and chipmunks persist.
Over 200 species of birds enlist to keep watch.
Broad-tailed hummingbirds, hairy woodpeckers, zone-tailed hawks,
common ravens, western bluebirds, and great horned owls.
Proof we are not lost. Proof we are not as repeating....

Rocks from space driving into our blue Moon. Yet.
Rocks from space have hit Earth many times.
People have not yet explored the red planet on foot.
We will be orbiting Venus, vicissitudes
when the message comes shredded of gloved letters
to be time mixed up.

For the first time children will understand
the concept of but the pilot has never landed this

rocket. Hello, I am Earth. I am the best planet in the solar system.
I want to remind you that you draw the world.

Thomas Osatchoff, together with family, is building a self-sustaining home near a waterfall in The Philippines. Recent work has appeared in *Adjacent Pineapple, Barzakh Magazine, In Parentheses*, and elsewhere.

Neighborhoods are Made of Moving Pieces
Dave Seter

A single Mom eats her son's unwanted bread crusts.
We may call this economy or something else.
What does the economist say when Moms economize
in other ways, save to send their children to college—

—across the ocean—where maple trees drink in water,
make sugar—and cast seeds into the wind, whirligig.
Trees only seems to stand still with cantilevered arms
reaching toward the sun, risking fracture—but—

we all travel through our sons and daughters.
Where we land? A matter of luck, seeding the family tree.

Dave Seter is the author of *Don't Sing to Me of Electric Fences*, due out from Cherry Grove Collections in 2021. His poems and critical works have appeared in *Paterson Literary Review, The Hopper, Raven Chronicles, Palaver, Confluence*, and other journals. He has received two Pushcart nominations. He is currently on the Board of Directors of the Marin Poetry Center. He earned his undergraduate degree in civil engineering from Princeton University and his graduate degree in humanities from Dominican University of California. Born in Chicago, he now lives in Sonoma County, California.

Reflections of My Father's Face
James Eric Watkins

Sometimes I see your face
when I walk slow by a window.

I follow your ghost
(or is it mine?). Our
eyes meet for single second.

And within this moment
the past and the present
the living and the dead
connect, like a wormhole
connects one place in space and time to another

conducted through a reflection
contained in a dimension
so small that it exists

within the thinness
of a pane of glass.

James Eric Watkins has dramatically performed his poetry at the Madison-Jefferson County (Indiana) Public Library, the University of Southern Indiana, and at Indiana University Southeast, as well as at the Village Lights Bookstore in Madison, Indiana and other venues. James' creative work has appeared in *Acorn, The Scioto Voice Newspaper, The Main Street Rag, Pegasus, Tipton Poetry Journal, Visions, Moments of the Soul* and many others.

Canyon de Chelly
Michael E. Strosahl

Inspired by the Mural Project photos by Ansel Adams and the story of the Navajo Nation who lives there

This is our home,
where the river you call Colorado
carved at the red rock,
waters turned to blood
with those lost
to the Long Walk,
when your government
burned down our hogans,
destroying our crops and peaches,
seizing our livestock
to move us
where they thought we should be,
overcrowded and amongst our enemies
at the Bosque Rodondo,
drinking from the Pecos
unsettling the spirits of the belly
of nearly all the *Dine'*.

This was not our home,
as our people walked weak,
fought daily with the Mescalero
and starved for the food
your governors promised
until their admitted failure,
when we were released
to go back,
reclaiming the canyon
and the waters that birthed us,
blue, green, brown and red.

This is our home.

Michael E. Strosahl is a midwestern river-born poet, originally from Moline, Illinois, now living in Jefferson City, Missouri. Besides several appearances in the *Tipton Poetry Journal*, Maik's work has appeared in *Flying Island, Bards Against Hunger* projects, on buses, in museums and online at *indianavoicejournal, poetrysuperhighway* and *projectagentorange*. Maik also has a weekly poetry column at the online blog *Moristotle & Company*.

Two Horses
Mary Shanley

She admitted to a close friendship
with the infamous literary outlaw,
Lucien Carr,

but she refused to speak about
their relationship with anyone.

She would only allow that she and Lucien
discussed Plato's Phaedrus, an ancient piece
of writing dating back to 370 b.c.

In the Phaedrus, Socrates compares
the life experience to that of a charioteer
holding the reins of two winged horses:

one ascends to higher aspects of our nature,
the other drags us down to the baser elements.

She both identified with this conflict and focused
on keeping the righteous horse in the ascendant.

But, because a human can only exert so much control
over the horses of fate,

it would only be a matter of time before
her inevitable collapse into the darker realm.

As the horse dragged her through the bottom rungs
of this horrific dimension, she encountered
spirits who were lost, who were screaming

and begging for release, as they were enchained
and hopeless. She was familiar with this terrifying
region of the underworld.

Periodically, fires would break out, and as she
stood next to the flames, she felt the horse ascending.

She grabbed the reins, and rode ever upward;
free from the shock and horror of the abyss.

She re-doubled her resolve to guide the horse

into the ascendant. The scariest part of her time
in darkness was knowing she could remain there,
but for the instincts of her righteous horse.

Mary Shanley is a poet/writer who lives in New York City. Her poetry is informed by the spiritual nature of life, the mysteries of life, the landscape of New York City and beyond. Four of her books have been published: *Hobo Code Poems* by Vox Pop Press; *Things They Left Behind*, *Poems for Faces* and *Mott Street Stories* and *Las Vegas Stories* by Side Street Press. Mary publishes online at: *Blaze Vox, Dream Noir, Underground Voices, Mobius, Radius, Mr. Bellers's Neighborhood, Blue Lake Review, Logos Journal, Hobo Camp Review, StepAway Magazine, Anak Sastra Journal, Shangra-la Magazine* and more. She was the Featured Poet on WBAI fmRadio NYC, and was nominated for a Pushcart Prize.

Ms. Waterman
Michele Penn Diaz

Ms. Waterman was the name
 of our school secretary

I thought it was
Miss Watermelon
        her hair was even red

My mom would steal smoke breaks with her
after dropping off us kids

When we caught her in the real world
        At a restaurant   or the drug store

It was as if a Clue suspect
        had escaped the game board
                to run some urgent errands

and uncomfortably, I thought:

Get back in there.

Michele Penn Diaz is a neurodivergent poet living in Portland, Oregon with her husband and an unruly schnauzer. In 2015, she received a BA in English from San Francisco State University. She works as a glorified receptionist and enjoys being surprised with peonies. She has forthcoming work in *Rust + Moth*.

The Watchman
Matthew Brennan

"That the Constables see every House shut up, and to be attended with Watchmen, which may keep them in . . . for the space of four Weeks."
   —Orders by the Lord Mayor, concerning the Plague, 1665

It's a chilly night as dark and still
as London's boneyard when the Deathcart comes
to dump the daily toll. The cart's heaped bodies—
purple and swollen, green with gangrene spots—
shine ghastly in the bellman's glaring torchlight.
The watchman's shift will last till 9 a.m.

Nothing stirs in the muddy street, not even
fleas buried in the fur of rats. All dogs
and cats have been butchered to stop the plague.
All the watchman hears is his own breathing.
Tonight the moon is down, but the red cross
that marks the door still glimmers like a gash.

No one's shown their face since Friday night
when women yelled for him to call the cart,
to carry off a maid they'd wrapped in rugs.
Then Monday afternoon, wailing escaped
an upstairs window; soon an angry man
was screaming for the cart again. Once there,
the carters knocked and knocked, louder each time.

So now it's the night watchman's turn again.
He stands as if in church. He fears what's next,
what's happened in the house and why it's mute.
At last, before dawn starts to lift the darkness,
he climbs up to the casement, cracks it open,
and calls inside. Hears nothing. Listens harder,
barely making out a metal tinkling,

and sees a simple latch, unhooked and swinging
in the breeze. Suddenly, the silence tolls
like Easter Sunday in the watchman's mind:
Hoisting upward to the ceiling hatch,
the family, leaving their beloved to rot,
had risen, Lazarus-like, from living death,

then crossed a row of rooftops and were gone.

Matthew Brennan's poems have appeared in *Sewanee Review, South Carolina Review, Notre Dame Review, Galway Review,* and others. His fifth collection, *One Life*, was published in 2016 (Lamar University Literary Press), and his sixth, *Snow in New York: New and Selected Poems*, is due in 2021. *The Colosseum Critical Introduction to Dana Gioia* was released last fall from Franciscan University Press. In 2017, after 32 years of teaching literature and poetry writing at Indiana State University, he retired and moved with his wife and two cats to Columbus, Ohio.

Sometimes, Thought
Jerry Jerome

Sometimes, thought fills full,
framed with flaming emotions, too full of itself.
Sometimes, thought puts its foot down
refusing to move.
Sometimes, I lean into a brilliant thought.
It moves away. I fall.

Jerry Jerome is the author of 50 published poems, from over 1,000 written due to laziness & vanity feelings. Numerous short stories, 3 novels, 1 screen play, & a memoir that tells of running political campaigns (*The Politic of Politics*) & becoming Deputy Mayor in the most corrupt upstate N.Y. village. Featured poet atB & N venues. Columbia College/Law School grad. Successful purveyor of commodities. He lives now in California.

O holy night
J. Lintu

You would have grown tired of me
as France of England
you wrapped so well in fine tissue and cord
me in the rough, brown paper of
butchers and cellared cheese.
Opening it was like the
cutting, breathy bolt of Christmas morning
shared by tumbling bunk-bed brothers. It was
too shocking a carol to hear what
beat within the box
and in the
inevitable ripping open, we
tore its bleeding stitches of ink and church water.
It skipped, just before the
severance, and bled dark, sticky sugar over our hands.
Sweet and stupid. That's what we
were. But like a
caroler with a single lung
I have learned what holiness means: to
sing during this cold, broken night and
still strain for the highest note without the aid of
star or gift. Or king.

Holy orders
J. Lintu

and I can do happy on 30 minutes a day
and I can hear my youngest: Daddy, don't save me
and I can sing from a blank hymnal, happily
and I can read Buddhists and cry, wanting a sucker
and I can lick my way toward that sweet red sea. If I
  want to cross it, I will
and I can turn a cashier's head still
and I can say I got money
and I can sit at table with wife, healed by tea, honey. No
  more needful thing than her bullet mind; being shot at
and I can pretend I'm St. Sebastian while my torso yet remains an
  egg-laden soufflé. Help me, doctor
and I can take pills, and untake them. I can
and I can wait for holiness, shaken and hard, ready to
  vomit if it all gets too pretty
and I can be both burrito and sauced, even without a
  movie and the mysterious Mexican friends I always want
and I can say hello middle-school cafeteria memories
and I can fight the good fight with all my might and
  laugh at the spiders fleeing from my mouth
and I can wear the friar costume and clap my hands without
  smiling at all, even though I am
and I could pray all day, if you'd like, without thinking of you once,
  holding you the whole while

J. Lintu's work has appeared in *Visio, The West Wind Review, The Penwood Review,* newversenews.com, *earthsongs*, and *Foxfold Press*, as well as forthcoming work in *Aji Magazine, Absolution*, and a chapbook-in-development from Impossible Press. An Associate Artist in Poetry under Joy Harjo at the Atlantic Center for the Arts, and a graduate of the Eastman School of Music, J. happily lives a few minutes away from Multnomah Falls in Oregon.

Working the Cologne Department at Macy's, 2010
James Croal Jackson

My olfactory nerve already overflooded with Acqua di Gio
on business cards beneath fluorescents, I did not expect

to run into my first love in the wilderness of Black Friday,
where hard rain was people. I sought a higher ground– escalator

to the bathroom to text my crush on my TracFone, until the arms
on my watch contorted a certain way. But my tarot cards flipped

when I recognized Kristen from afar, both of us unsure,
unlike in fifth grade, on the bus to Mohican, she slept

beside me, her hair fire on my shoulder, strobe lights of a confused
adolescence that entire week. Camp ended when everyone

contracted poison ivy. How to scratch the mind until snapping
back into self– in that present, years later, I thought she might be

fate and, thus, planned a coffee date, but because I did not
carve the path I wanted to take, winter came. And went.

James Croal Jackson (he/him) is a Filipino-American poet. He has a chapbook, *The Frayed Edge of Memory* (Writing Knights Press, 2017), and poems in *San Antonio Review, Sampsonia Way,* and *Pacifica*. He edits *The Mantle Poetry* (themantlepoetry.com). He works in film production in Pittsburgh, Pennsylvania. (jamescroaljackson.com)

Coronavirus Tutorial

Cameron Morse

Heat haunted body heat haunt,
let's begin with you
trapping sunshine in your dreamcatcher
of photosynthesis, your mash

of molars and bicuspids.
Let's begin with the thermogram
of an ice-skater. Are you not in your flesh meat
also angelic? Eat,

fell child, gnaw lettuce leaves
and caterpillars alike. The earth will
not requite the dark-eyed
marshmallow. If you want to arrive

at the virion, first don the peplos
of the Mediterranean, shrug
off your shoulder strap, kick off
your sandals and slip into the salt mirror

sheen of seaweed. Somewhere
in the depths of your body you may
find an agreeable host
for the starry-eyed saber-toothed

nimbus-eater that will gumball
your lungs, gum up the gear shaft
in a endless succession
of cranks, crises.

Cameron Morse Morse lives with his wife Lili and two children in Independence, Missouri. His poems have been published in numerous magazines, including *New Letters*, *Bridge Eight*, *Portland Review* and *South Dakota Review*. His first collection, *Fall Risk*, won Glass Lyre Press's 2018 Best Book Award. His latest is *Baldy* (Spartan Press, 2020). He holds an MFA from the University of Kansas City—Missouri and serves as Senior Reviews editor at *Harbor Review* and Poetry editor at *Harbor Editions*. For more information, check out his Facebook page or website.

Cartoon Character
Diane Webster

The man is a cartoon-channel character
chattering away in voices not his own
to cover thickly-clad person beneath
who obsesses every minor detail to death,
to death like hand-painted coyote
falling to the desert floor
with a boulder flattening him to paper
fluttering into a camper's fire to burn
and dive into nearest pond
where piranhas rip teeth marks
all over his body as he limps
down the road only to smash
into an ACME truck
as TV screen fades to black
and again and again we laugh
as weary as the coyote
as we bare our teeth
reflected back in computer screen,
a ghost we allow to haunt.

Prize Illusion
Diane Webster

I habitat this fog lying across me
like an effervescent mantle
dissolving me into grayness
so people shadows pass me
in a hide-and-seek game
where I am always the victor.

Always seeing but never seen
from two-way mirror
swirling thicker or thinner
depending on my clarity.
But sometimes I am too gray,
too comfortable with this foggy mass,
and when I grasp a person's hand,
he jerks away startled
by my touch so invisible
he flees, and I am blind.

Not darkness blind
but muffled almost seeing light
if I could open my eyes wide enough
if I could stumble free
or wait long enough for sunshine
to fade my cloud and slip it away
like a magician's cloak
leaving me the prize illusion.

Diane Webster's goal is to remain open to poetry ideas in everyday life, nature or an overheard phrase and to write. Diane, who lives in Colorado, enjoys the challenge of transforming images into words to fit her poems. Her work has appeared in *Philadelphia Poets, Old Red Kimono, Home Planet News Online* and other literary magazines.

Worlds

C.T. Holte

I know little about auras,
though a friend who said he did
and was also a respected
Volvo mechanic with his own shop
once said I had a good one.

Another fellow whom I never met
was able to interact with
supersensible worlds–
or said so in his book,
which I gave up halfway through
because it was going somewhere
I had no need to go.
I do not know if he had an aura,
or how many books he sold
at his self-promoted lectures.

However, a row of flowering plums
along our morning walk
is in radiant bloom this week,
so gorgeous that I stopped
to take a picture of the largest one
while the dog stopped next to another.

The old man in the too-large overcoat
slouched on the concrete bench
at the bus stop across the road
conversing quite loudly with himself
(or perhaps with a supersensible world)
may not have been aware of us
or the dog or the trees.
I silently willed him to share
the blessing of the otherworldly aura
of myriad plum-pink blossoms.

C.T. Holte was born in Minnesota before color TV; grew up playing under bridges, along creeks, and in cornfields; went to lots of school; and has (mostly) enjoyed gigs as teacher, writer, editor, and some less wordy things. Recently transplanted from California to New Mexico, by way of Arizona, he is enjoying the fiery chiles and sunsets. He tends to write about trees, water, and special people. His poetry has appeared or is pending in places like *Words, Touch, California Quarterly, Survival* (Poets Speak, vol. 5), *The Raven's Perch, Songs of Eretz Poetry Review, The Daily Drunk, Origami Poems Project, Pensive, The Rainbow Poems,* and *Better than Starbucks*, and has been hung from trees to celebrate the Rio Grande Bosque.

Getting an Education
Theresa Monteiro

Last night, reading,
I came across the word *thistle,*
but I've forgotten the context
because I couldn't, and can't,
call up the image of a thistle. I feel
this lack in myself—like the shame
of never understanding
imaginary numbers or what chemists mean
when they talk about a mole.
Mrs. Clark was childless, broken,
and this girl kept asking,
what's a mole? Six point zero two
times ten to the twenty-third power,
of course. An unimaginable number but not
an imaginary number so I try
to imagine a mole of thistles but can only recall
like the down of a thistle which is not
the thistle itself.

Mrs. Clark, I understand now,
at wakes, wanting to reach
inside the caskets—to give the bodies
reassuring pats, mumble to them
a mole of motherly things.
The rooms choke on lilies,
carnations, baby's breath, small purple blooms
like pom-poms, and now it comes back to me:
You will know them by their fruits.

Theresa Monteiro lives in New Hampshire with her husband and six children. She is a former teacher and holds an MFA from the University of New Hampshire. She has had poems published in *The American Journal of Poetry, River Heron Review, Pittsburgh Poetry Journal, Black Fork Review, Good Fat Poetry, Silver Needle Press*, and forthcoming in *The Meadow* and *Presence*. She received the Dick Shea Memorial Prize for poetry in 2019.

Terms of Service
Michael Jones

Apron on, she lays out
almonds and nonpareils;
he uses his remaining hand
to set the table. Behind them stands
the altar they dedicate
to all who've died in any war;
they refuse to prefer,
like any IED.

Michael Jones has taught in Oakland, California public schools since 1990. His poetry has appeared widely in journals, *Atlanta Review, Beloit Poetry Journal, Confrontation, DMQ Review*, etc., and in a chapbook, *Moved* (Kattywompus, 2016).

An Error in Judgment
Alan Cohen

The book split open
Like a pumpkin, cleaved by an axe,
Like a pinata,
And the characters spilled in a golden stream,
Glowing in the cold autumn air among the leaves.
I on my blanket, shivering with delight,
Almost beheld the whole of it,
Nearly fixed it indelible in my ageless inward gaze,
Such a wealth was mine--
I who had come to study, not to learn a trade.
My teachers bade me rest my gaze on a part of the whole —

On the pumpkin, the axe, the atmosphere, the characters, the season.
I should have chosen the honey, that golden essence,
Caught it in crystal goblets to display on my mantelpiece through the long winter;
But I was young and omnipotent
And I chose to study the model for the characters,
The measure of all things,
Man the ruler, man the timepiece, and failures in his delicate mechanism.
But as I broke him into ever smaller and more delicate components
Spreading his molecules about my room, numbered and ordered,
My spirit flagged;
And then, as I took up the molecules, one by one,
Suddenly urgent, I saw their deformity,
Knew the betrayal,
And faltered into the war,
Gentamycin and methotrexate
My torpedo and machine gun.

At Shavouos, the Jewish celebration of the fall harvest,
We dip apples in honey, say a blessing,
And eat them both together.
At Halloween, in America,
We submerge our heads in a bowl of water and take an apple between our teeth.

The time has come
To embrace the vision of my childhood,
To loosen my death grasp
On the browning core of an eaten apple
(Though I know the core contains the seeds).
It is the creation, not the creator,
It is the vision, not its inspiration
That is lovable and deserving of protection.
I celebrate the honey of my youth

Alan Cohen was a poet before beginning his career as a Primary Care MD, teacher, and manager, and has been living a full and varied life. He's been writing poems for 60 years, is beginning now to share some of his discoveries, and has had 114 poems published in 58 venues over the past 8 months. He's been married to Anita for 41 years, and they've been in Eugene, Oregon these past 11.

Who We Are
Jonathan Bracker

I am two people. How about you,
Aren't you two people, too?

Think about it.
No matter what your age,
There may be two of you:
One courageous, confronting
Dragons perhaps daily, and one
Frightened, ready to rush pell-mell
The hell out of any dragon-infested
Territory, tail between its legs.

It is good that, being two,
We are able to choose what to do.

And yet we are sometimes one.
You feel we are, don't you?

Aren't you sometimes only a groundhog
Or hedgehog doing what naturally
You do, unaware how humans
Write books called The Tragic View
Of Life or read such books rather
Than deal with the dragons you see in the meadow
As you munch slugs and grubs, unconcerned?
And aren't you glad you are?

Poems by **Jonathan Bracker** have appeared in *The New Yorker, Poetry Northwest* and other periodicals, and in eight collections, the latest of which, from Seven Kitchens Press, is *Attending Junior High*. He lives in San Francisco and is the editor of *Bright Cages: Selected Poems of Christopher Morley* (University of Pennsylvania Press: 1965; reissued 2018); co-author with Mark I. Wallach of *Christopher Morley* (Twayne: 1976); and editor of *A Little Patch of Shepherd's Thyme: Prose Passages Of Thomas Hardy Arranged As Verse* (Moving Finger Press: 2013).

The Class on Emily Dickinson
Hamilton Salsich

The professor said her poems
are full of surprises,
but he himself seemed steady and consistent.
His slides were systematic,
and his words worked in an efficient way,
with no suddenness,
no shocking phrases.
The leaves outside were swirling
in surprising ways,
and my thoughts
were messily throwing themselves around,
but all was symmetry and smoothness
in this class about a woman
who made poems
like lit-up,
startling
storms.

Hamilton Salsich is a teacher, husband, and father of four who lives in Connecticut and has been published in a number of journals, most recently *Common Ground Review, White Pelican Review, Fox Cry Review, The Paper Street Journal, Amarolla, Briar Cliff Review,* and *Tiny Seed Literary Journal.*

The equinox and the solstice
Akshaya Pawaskar

The caliginous sky grows
like a forest of diamonds.
The poet harvests poems
from this field of dazzling stars.
Our world shrunk like
a wall to which the lizard clings
yet vision traverses through the dusk
to see the distant light.
It is the darkness that equalizes
our skin, our tired bones
our minds dimmed
by Valium,
pecking order surrendered
to a need for sleep,
a caesura.
God scoffs at us
under the hunter's moon,
when we hunt for the game
knowing we have become it,
a dart for a dart.
Then the solstice arrives,
a slow culmination of autumn greys
the dead leaf reverently falling
to the tree's feet
which meditates naked
into the wintry evenings.
The sun retires to bed, early
lending its shine
to the obsidian planet
whose colors
then come to life.
If only we could learn
from him to not pinch pennies
while sharing ones
own brightness, that
does not diminish but
only thrives.

We then wait patiently for
the Equinox,

It is a coin midair.
What did you wish for,
Heads or tails? It asks.
The night finally equals the day.
It is once again a time
for vernal starts.

Akshaya Pawaskar is a doctor practicing in India and poetry is her passion. Her poems have been published in *Tipton Poetry Journal, the punch magazine, Shards, The Blue Nib, North of Oxford, Indian Ruminations, Rock & Sling* among many others. She had been chosen as the winner of ekphrastic poetry competition 2020 by Craven arts council, third place winner of Poetry Matters Project contest 2020 and second place winner of *The Blue Nib* chapbook contest 2018.

Wholly Holy
Karla Linn Merrifield

The generative scaffold
of this tribute poem
is the C chord, easy,
then the F chord, hard.
Mr. Waits chooses
to play flattened,
but it's not his badly tuned
guitar, it's his deliberate dissonance.

So, like Tom, I pick gingerly,
unconventionally jumping
as if catapulting on adverbs
from the low E to D string
on his G chord , hoping
happily, haplessly,
I don't fall in love
with him or anybody else,

but his voice in my gravelly tones
at the end of forgotten nights—
cigarettes, booze, maybe
weed-infused, maybe pheromonally
induced karma of lovingly
lonesome bar-stool longing
along the fretboard toward
hits the profound sound hole of our guitars.

Let's search these measures in Time
for all the lost places in our lives.

Karla Linn Merrifield lives in Florida and has had 800+ poems appear in dozens of journals and anthologies. She has 14 books to her credit. Following her 2018 *Psyche's Scroll* (Poetry Box Select) is the 2019 full-length *Athabaskan Fractal: Poems of the Far North* from Cirque Press. She is currently at work on a poetry collection, *My Body the Guitar*, inspired by famous guitarists and their guitars to be published by Before Your Quiet Eyes Holograph Series (Rochester, NY) in late 2021.

White Flag
Leslie Schultz

for Edna St. Vincent Millay

Surrender or retreat:
the snowy tail of a deer who runs from the hunter?

Mere ruse, as tricky
to interpret as an empty page?
Simply orchid-like loveliness,
an albino iris in a marshy place or a starry swamp lily?

Once it signaled conjugal harmony,
an artist's truce with the body's imperatives.

From the shelter of fine old trees, in her small writing shed,
Edna St. Vincent Millay would decide to stop
burning her candle at both ends, to accept
her human cry for food and rest—

still struggling to stay, cloudlike, adrift on azure visions,
reluctant to partake of earthbound needs—she admitted

her weakness only to her husband. She'd tie, they say,
a white handkerchief to a doorknob or window ledge,
up at Steepletop, and he'd carry over something
sustaining and delicious, knowing that for a few minutes

she would surrender her penciled words,
allow his advance of love.

Leslie Schultz (Northfield, Minnesota) is the author of three collections of poetry, *Still Life with Poppies: Elegies* (Kelsay Books, 2016), *Cloud Song* (Kelsay Books, 2018)., and *Concertina* (Kelsay Books, 2019) Her poetry has appeared most recently in *Poet Lore, North Dakota Quarterly, Able Muse, Blue Unicorn Journal, Light, Mezzo Cammin, Swamp Lily Review, Third Wednesday, The Madison Review, The Midwest Quarterly, The Orchards Poetry Journal,* and *The Wayfarer*; in the sidewalks of Northfield; and in a chapbook, *Living Room* (Midwestern Writers' Publishing House). She received a Pushcart Prize nomination in 2017 and has had three winning poems in the Maria W. Faust sonnet contest (2013, 2016, 2019). Schultz posts poems, photographs, and essays on her website: www.winonamedia.net.

Rip

Ken Craft

Upon seeing Confederate flags outside some Maine households.

Maybe it was wrong, wishing I were Rip Van Winkle
so I could sleep four orange years away, wake, and shout,
"This, too, has passed!" to the ticker tape masses.
But the folk tale fantasy of it all was dismissed by a friend labeling
my silence "moral cowardice." He counseled waking and woke,

running past the Sleepy Hollow barbershop's pole of blue, blood,
and white; getting the cynicism trimmed from my eyebrows,
having the indifference brushed from my beard. Might it
be too late by then, I asked, swiping sand motes from my eyes,
Q-Tipping lost opportunities from my ears?

Might I hear barking men, see boorish salutes, witness crisp
Stars and Bars flapping on flag poles along either side of
Main Street in this Free State of Maine, which buried over
7,000 Union dead? "Yes," he replied. "And return to another
country entirely. One no amount of sleep could salvage."

Ken Craft 's poems have appeared in *The Writer's Almanac, Verse Daily, One, South Florida Poetry Journal, Pedestal Magazine,* and numerous other journals and e-zines. He lives in Maine and is the author of two collections of poetry, *Lost Sherpa of Happiness* (Kelsay Books) and *The Indifferent World* (FutureCycle Press). His third collection, *Reincarnation & Other Stimulants,* will appear in 2021.

Deloris

Mary Hills Kuck

Every so often Deloris, married at the prodding of her church
when she found herself swelling the third time for a third man,
leaves the tangled city of Kingston and her board house with its
zinc roof in its clamorous yard where she is surrounded by her husband,
in-laws, her daughter almost finished with high school, and her
taxi-driver second son, when times are hard and he has no woman.

Deloris leaves, on the country bus or in said taxi, for the bush
country of her childhood. Farmers chop at scallion
on the hillside and goats roam the rises looking for sparse
grass to fatten themselves.

Deloris settles into her deceased mother's concrete block house,
which she rehabs visit-by-visit. She views torrents of rain through
a fogged glass door, music thrumming from a radio spliced
to a lone electric wire.

She talks to her spirits--to her mother who willed her this house,
to her father who loved her too much, then sent her to Kingston,
to her country son raised by her mother, and chopped into bits
by machete. They visit for days in the rain and steam.

[This poem was first published in *Fever Grass: A collection of New and Established Caribbean Poets, Book 2*]

Having retired from teaching English and Communications, first in the US and for many years in Jamaica, Mary Hills Kuck now lives with her family in Massachusetts. She has received a Pushcart Prize Nomination and her poems have appeared in *Connecticut River Review, Hamden Chronicle, SIMUL: Lutheran Voices in Poetry, Caduceus, The Jamaica Observer Bookends, Fire Stick: A Collection of New & Established Caribbean Poets, the Aurorean, Tipton Poetry Journal, Burningwood Literary Journal, Slant* and *Main Street Rag* (both forthcoming), and others.

Review: The Keeping by Linda Neal Reising
Reviewed by Dan Carpenter

Title: *The Keeping*

Author: Linda Neal Reising

Year: August 20, 2020

Publisher: Finishing Line Press

There are red Americans and there are red Americans, and there's nobody like the culturally assimilated but ethnically aware to do the distinction justice. When the observer happens to be a poet, the rich and rueful shadings of that compromised inheritance can be conveyed in a snapshot.

"Like Wild Paints" could stand as the signature entry in Linda Neal Reising's pungent new collection for several reasons, most of all for its capture of the subject-object kinship in her account from adolescence of a ballgame between her Oklahoma school of "bleached" Native Americans and an Indian institution whose athletes "gleam(ed) like copper kettles in sunlight."

> They never spoke to us girls – giggling and flirting
> on the rickety bleachers – or even smiled,
> eyes always averted, downcast, except
> when they stepped up to bat.
> Then they held their chins high –
> warriors or gods or both – watched
> as the ball hurled toward the plate,
> then sent it orbiting into brambles
> beyond the fence before galloping
> the bases like wild Paints,
> their manes whipping behind,
> with one thought – to run,
> run!

Again, so much here. Empathy along with introspection. Stark succinctness narrowing down to a closing that strikes like a BB between the eyes. Rhythm subtle as sweaty male shoulders flexing before a clueless girl in the grandstand. Even more subtle and evocative – the call-out of injustice. Always, and not always distant, the ominous drums.

What's remarkable about "Like Wild Paints" is its explicitness in addressing the author's racial heritage as a social issue, something that is kept well below the often hard and hazardous surface of the four dozen companion poems of which it is nevertheless representative in those several respects. Reising is decidedly not a polemical poet, and not one to cheat herself or her readers out of unadulterated experience of the pleasures, tragedy, horror, humor and grudging consolations of the world as she finds it.

From "An Educated Woman Explains Why She Likes Bluegrass":

> *Because a mandolin quivers,*
> *a timid soul, fluttering*
> *like the wings of a blackbird*
> *trapped inside a stone chimney.*

From "Taking Leave," about the real-life escape of an octopus from a zoo aquarium:

> *. . . if he ever wished to once again*
> *hold the sea's immensity in his arms.*

Reising's command of metaphor, simile and personification is on display throughout this vivacious collection, to the point where imagery itself becomes the subject – and slyly so.

Her tribute to the late nature poet Mary Oliver, "Mary's Eyes," teems with blackberries "like garnet earrings," mushrooms "sheltered by wide-brimmed sun hats" and such, then slams closed with lines that wryly serve to put imagery and the imagist in their place:

> *I want to see with Mary's eyes*
> *all of nature's metaphors,*
> *see them so clearly*
> *I can let them go.*

Nature, memories of home and the resilience of women comprise the book's three thematic sections. The arrangement affords a full display of Reising's dramatic and descriptive chops as well as an engaging glimpse of her biography, dating to the mid-20th Century, and the lives of dear and not-so-dear figures covering far more years.

Melancholy, often soured to bitterness, attaches to a number of these accounts.

There's none other than Mickey Mantle, a schoolmate of the poet's dad and, spared the draft that sent his classmate to Korea,

> *Pumped his "bad" leg around major league bases,*
> *Came in sliding, and made it home safe.*

There's the sixth-grade Carnival King to the poet's Queen, whose suffering from domestic abuse became known when

> *he put a gun to the chest of his ex-Marine*
> *father, one red carnation blooming*
> *where his heart should have been.*

It is potent stuff Laura Neal Reising pours for us in this follow-up to her first publication, an award-winning chapbook from the same publisher, titled *Re-Writing Family History*. I defy you to read "Homecoming," drawn from a chance encounter at a salad bar with a long-ago sexual attacker, without doubling your fists and wishing that fork had found the bastard's neck instead of that pickled beet lifted bleeding onto a plate.

Ah, but Reising's women take their sustenance, gather their strength, outlast their tormentors, outgrow the gamesmanship of enforced femininity, and carry however heavily or lightly "the sin of being Eve's daughters". They labor to push forth babies that will die as youths on a battlefield, they make poetry of their bodies in a Jazzercise class at the high school and a Monday night dance at Miss Audrey's Pickin' Parlor. They let go in a karate class with

> *The primal panther scream*

knowing that

> *It is the hardest lesson for women –*
> *This finding voice.*

We're all fortunate so many have put in the hard work. We are blessed, as well as challenged, to have this quality product from an Indiana transplant for our keeping.

A fiction and non-fiction writer, as well as a poet, **Linda Neal Reising** is a native of Oklahoma and a member of the Western Cherokee Nation. Linda has been published in numerous journals and anthologies, including *And Know This Place:Poetry of Indiana; Storm Country; Lost on Route 66:Tales from the Mother Road;* and *Fruitflesh: Seeds of Inspiration for Women Who Write*. In 2009 she won the Judith Siegel Pearson Writing Award, and in 2012 she was named the winner of the *Writers Digest* Poetry Competition. Her winning work appeared in *Writers Digest* and an anthology of the winning poems.

Dan Carpenter is a board member of Brick Street Poetry Inc. and the author of two collections of poetry and two books of non-fiction. He has contributed poems and stories to many journals and anthologies. He blogs at dancarpenterpoet.wordpress.com.

Editor

Barry Harris is editor of the *Tipton Poetry Journal* and three anthologies by Brick Street Poetry: *Mapping the Muse: A Bicentennial Look at Indiana Poetry; Words and Other Wild Things* and *Cowboys & Cocktails:Poems from the True Grit Saloon.* He has published one poetry collection, *Something At The Center.*

Married and father of two grown sons, Barry lives in Brownsburg, Indiana and is retired from Eli Lilly and Company.

His poetry has appeared in *Kentucky Review, Valparaiso Poetry Review, Grey Sparrow, Silk Road Review, Saint Ann's Review, Boston Literary Magazine, Night Train, Silver Birch Press, Flying Island, Awaken Consciousness, Writers' Bloc,* and *Red-Headed Stepchild.* One of his poems was on display at the National Museum of Sport and another is painted on a barn in Boone County, Indiana as part of Brick Street Poetry's Word Hunger public art project. His poems are also included in these anthologies: *From the Edge of the Prairie; Motif 3: All the Livelong Day;* and *Twin Muses: Art and Poetry.*

He graduated a long time ago with a major in English from Ball State University.

Contributor Biographies

Tobi Alfier is a multiple Pushcart nominee and multiple Best of the Net nominee. *Slices of Alice & Other Character Studies* was published by Cholla Needles Press. *Symmetry: earth and sky* was published by Main Street Rag. She is co-editor of *San Pedro River Review*(www.bluehorsepress.com) and lives in California.

Poems by **Jonathan Bracker** have appeared in *The New Yorker, Poetry Northwest* and other periodicals, and in eight collections, the latest of which, from Seven Kitchens Press, is *Attending Junior High*. He lives in San Francisco and is the editor of *Bright Cages: Selected Poems of Christopher Morley* (University of Pennsylvania Press: 1965; reissued 2018); co-author with Mark I. Wallach of *Christopher Morley* (Twayne: 1976); and editor of *A Little Patch of Shepherd's Thyme: Prose Passages Of Thomas Hardy Arranged As Verse* (Moving Finger Press: 2013).

Matthew Brennan's poems have appeared in *Sewanee Review, South Carolina Review, Notre Dame Review, Galway Review*, and others. His fifth collection, *One Life*, was published in 2016 (Lamar University Literary Press), and his sixth, *Snow in New York: New and Selected Poems*, is due in 2021. *The Colosseum Critical Introduction to Dana Gioia* was released last fall from Franciscan University Press. In 2017, after 32 years of teaching literature and poetry writing at Indiana State University, he retired and moved with his wife and two cats to Columbus, Ohio.

Born in Perugia, Italy, a graduate of the Catholic University of the Sacred Heart (Milan, Italy) and of Mills College (Oakland, California), **Simona Carini** writes poetry and nonfiction and has been published in various venues, in print and online, including *Intima - A Journal of Narrative Medicine, Italian Americana, Sheila-Na-Gig Online, the Journal of Humanistic Mathematics, the American Journal of Nursing, Star 82 Review*. She lives in Northern California with her husband and works as a data scientist at an academic research institution. Her website is https://simonacarini.com.

Dan Carpenter is a board member of Brick Street Poetry Inc. and the author of two collections of poetry and two books of non-fiction. He has contributed poems and stories to many journals and anthologies. He blogs at dancarpenterpoet.wordpress.com.

Alan Cohen was a poet before beginning his career as a Primary Care MD, teacher, and manager, and has been living a full and varied life. He's been writing poems for 60 years, is beginning now to share some of his discoveries, and has had 114 poems published in 58 venues over the past 8 months. He's been married to Anita for 41 years, and they've been in Eugene, Oregon these past 11.

Ken Craft 's poems have appeared in *The Writer's Almanac, Verse Daily, One, South Florida Poetry Journal, Pedestal Magazine,* and numerous other journals and e-zines. He lives in Maine and is the author of two collections of poetry, *Lost Sherpa of Happiness* (Kelsay Books) and *The Indifferent World* (FutureCycle Press). His third collection, *Reincarnation & Other Stimulants*, will appear in 2021.

Michele Penn Diaz is a neurodivergent poet living in Portland, Oregon with her husband and an unruly schnauzer. In 2015, she received a BA in English from San Francisco State University. She works as a glorified receptionist and enjoys being surprised with peonies. She has forthcoming work in *Rust + Moth*.

Diane Glancy is professor emerita at Macalester College. Currently, she teaches in the low-residency MFA program at Carlow University in Pittsburgh. Her latest poetry book, *Island of the Innocent, a Consideration of the Book of Job*, was published by Turtle Point Press in 2020. *A Line of Driftwood, a story of Ada Blackjack* is forthcoming from Turtle Point in 2021. Broadleaf Press will publish a collection of nonfiction in 2021, *Still Moving, How the Road, the Land and the Sacred Shape a Life*. Her awards and other books are on her website www.dianeglancy.com

G Timothy Gordon lives in Las Cruces, New Mexico. His eighth book, *Dream Wind*, was published December 2019 (Spirit-of-the-Ram Press). Work appears in *AGNI, American Literary Review, Cincinnati Review, Kansas Quarterly, Louisville Review, Mississippi Review, New York Quarterly, Phoebe, RHINO, Sonora Review, Texas Observer*, among others. *Everything Speaking Chinese* received Riverstone Books' Poetry Book Prize. Recognitions include NEA & NEH Fellowships, residencies, and several Pushcart nominations. His chapbook, *Empty Heaven, Empty Earth*, will be published Spring-Summer 2021. He divides professional & personal lives among Asia, the Southwest, & Maine.

An editor, writer, and poet, **Charles Grosel** grew up in the suburbs of Cleveland, Ohio. After stints on both the West and East Coasts, he now lives in Arizona with his wife and daughter. He studied English literature at Yale University and fiction writing at the University of California at Davis, where he was a Regent's Fellow. To earn a living, he has been a teacher, editor, trainer, and ghost writer, among other jobs, but through it all he has kept at his true vocation, writing poetry and fiction. He has published stories in journals such as *Western Humanities Review, Fiction Southeast, Water-Stone, and The MacGuffin*, as well as poems in *Slate, The Threepenny Review, Poet Lore, Cream City Review,* and *Harpur Palate*. Charles owns the communications firm, Write for Success (write4success.net). *The Sound of Rain Without Water*, a chapbook of poems, came out in December 2020.

Shakiba Hashemi is an Iranian-American poet, painter and teacher living in Southern California. She is a bilingual poet, and writes in English and Farsi. She holds a BFA in Drawing and Painting from Laguna College of Art and Design. Her work has recently appeared in *Atlanta Review* and is forthcoming in *I-70 Review* and the New York Quarterly Anthology *Without a Doubt: poems illuminating faith.*

C.T. Holte was born in Minnesota before color TV; grew up playing under bridges, along creeks, and in cornfields; went to lots of school; and has (mostly) enjoyed gigs as teacher, writer, editor, and some less wordy things. Recently transplanted from California to New Mexico, by way of Arizona, he is enjoying the fiery chiles and sunsets. He tends to write about trees, water, and special people. His poetry has appeared or is pending in places like *Words, Touch, California Quarterly, Survival* (Poets Speak, vol. 5), *The Raven's Perch, Songs of Eretz Poetry Review, The Daily Drunk, Origami Poems Project, Pensive, The Rainbow Poems,* and *Better than Starbucks*, and has been hung from trees to celebrate the Rio Grande Bosque.

James Croal Jackson (he/him) is a Filipino-American poet. He has a chapbook, *The Frayed Edge of Memory* (Writing Knights Press, 2017), and poems in *San Antonio Review, Sampsonia Way*, and *Pacifica*. He edits *The Mantle Poetry* (themantlepoetry.com). He works in film production in Pittsburgh, Pennsylvania. (jamescroaljackson.com)

Jennifer Ruth Jackson is an award-winning poet and fiction writer living in Wisconsin whose work has appeared in *Red Earth Review, Banshee*, and more. She runs a blog for disabled and neurodivergent creatives called *The Handy, Uncapped Pen* from an apartment she shares with her husband. Follow her on Twitter @jenruthjackson.

Jerry Jerome is the author of 50 published poems, from over 1,000 written due to laziness & vanity feelings. Numerous short stories, 3 novels, 1 screen play, & a memoir that tells of running political campaigns (*The Politic of Politics*) & becoming Deputy Mayor in the most corrupt upstate N.Y. village. Featured poet atB & N venues. Columbia College/Law School grad. Successful purveyor of commodities. He lives now in California.

Michael Jones has taught in Oakland, California public schools since 1990. His poetry has appeared widely in journals, *Atlanta Review, Beloit Poetry Journal, Confrontation, DMQ Review*, etc., and in a chapbook, *Moved* (Kattywompus, 2016).

Robert S. King lives in Athens, Georgia, where he serves on the board of FutureCycle Press and edits *Good Works Review*. His poems have appeared in hundreds of magazines, including *Atlanta Review, California Quarterly, Chariton Review, Hollins Critic, Kenyon Review, Main Street Rag, Midwest Quarterly, Negative Capability, Southern Poetry Review*, and *Spoon River Poetry Review*. He has published eight poetry collections, most recently *Diary of the Last Person on Earth* (Sybaritic Press 2014), *Developing a Photograph of God* (Glass Lyre Press, 2014), and *Messages from Multiverses* (Duck Lake Books, 2020). His personal website is www.robertsking.info.

Having retired from teaching English and Communications, first in the US and for many years in Jamaica, **Mary Hills Kuck** now lives with her family in Massachusetts. She has received a Pushcart Prize Nomination and her poems have appeared in *Connecticut River Review, Hamden Chronicle, SIMUL: Lutheran Voices in Poetry, Caduceus, The Jamaica Observer Bookends, Fire Stick: A Collection of New & Established Caribbean Poets, the Aurorean, Tipton Poetry Journal, Burningwood Literary Journal, Slant* and *Main Street Rag* (both forthcoming), and others.

Charlene Langfur lives in Palm Springs, California, and is a southern Californian, an organic gardener, a Syracuse University Graduate Writing Fellow. Her most recent publications include poems in *Emrys, Inlandia, North Dakota Quarterly*, and a series of poems forthcoming in *Weber – The Contemporary West*.

Bruce Levine, a 2019 Pushcart Prize Poetry Nominee, has spent his life as a writer of fiction and poetry and as a music and theatre professional. Over 300 of his works are published in over 25 on-line journals including *Ariel Chart, Friday Flash Fiction, Literary Yard;* over 30 print books including *Poetry Quarterly, Haiku Journal, Dual Coast Magazine*, and his shows have been produced in New York and around the country. Six eBooks are available from Amazon.com. His work is dedicated to the loving memory of his late wife, Lydia Franklin. He lives in New York with his dog, Daisy. Visit him at www.brucelevine.com.

J. Lintu's work has appeared in *Visio, The West Wind Review, The Penwood Review*, newversenews.com, *earthsongs*, and *Foxfold Press*, as well as forthcoming work in *Aji Magazine, Absolution*, and a chapbook-in-development from Impossible Press. An Associate Artist in Poetry under Joy Harjo at the Atlantic Center for the Arts, and a graduate of the Eastman School of Music, J. happily lives a few minutes away from Multnomah Falls in Oregon.

A retired educator living in a small town in eastern Oregon, **Jack e Lorts** has appeared widely, if infrequently, over the past 50+ years such places as *Arizona Quarterly, Kansas Quarterly, English Journal, Chiron Review, Tipton Poetry Journal, verse daily* among others. Author of three previous chapbooks, his *The Love Songs of Epram Pratt* appeared in 2019 from Uttered Chaos Press.

Ken Meisel is a poet and psychotherapist, a 2012 Kresge Arts Literary Fellow, a Pushcart Prize nominee and the author of eight books of poetry. His most recent books are: *Our Common Souls: New & Selected Poems of Detroit* (Blue Horse Press: 2020) and *Mortal Lullabies* (FutureCycle Press: 2018). Meisel has recent work in *Concho River Review, I-70 Review, San Pedro River Review,* and *Rabid Oak*. Ken lives in Dearborn, Michigan.

Karla Linn Merrifield lives in Florida and has had 800+ poems appear in dozens of journals and anthologies. She has 14 books to her credit. Following her 2018 *Psyche's Scroll* (Poetry Box Select) is the 2019 full-length *Athabaskan Fractal: Poems of the Far North* from Cirque Press. She is currently at work on a poetry collection, *My Body the Guitar*, inspired by famous guitarists and their guitars to be published by Before Your Quiet Eyes Holograph Series (Rochester, NY) in late 2021.

Theresa Monteiro lives in New Hampshire with her husband and six children. She is a former teacher and holds an MFA from the University of New Hampshire. She has had poems published in *The American Journal of Poetry, River Heron Review, Pittsburgh Poetry Journal, Black Fork Review, Good Fat Poetry, Silver Needle Press*, and forthcoming in *The Meadow* and *Presence*. She received the Dick Shea Memorial Prize for poetry in 2019.

George Moore's poetry has appeared in *The Atlantic, North American Review, Colorado Review, Orion, Arc, Tipton Poetry Journal* and *Stand*. His most recent collections are *Children's Drawings of the Universe* (Salmon Poetry 2015) and *Saint Agnes Outside the Walls* (FurureCycle 2016). He is a seven-time Pushcart Prize nominee, and finalist for The National Poetry Series. His work was recently shortlisted for the Bailieborough Poetry Prize and long-listed for both the Gregory O'Donoghue and Ginkgo Poetry Prizes. Retired from the University of Colorado, Boulder, he lives on the south shore of Nova Scotia.

Julie L. Moore is the author of four poetry collections, including, most recently, *Full Worm Moon*, which won a 2018 Woodrow Hall Top Shelf Award and received honorable mention for the Conference on Christianity and Literature's 2018 Book of the Year. A Best of the Net and five-time Pushcart Prize nominee, she has also published poetry in *Alaska Quarterly Review, African American Review, Image, New Ohio Review, Poetry Daily, Prairie Schooner, The Southern Review,* and *Verse Daily*. Her work likewise has appeared in several anthologies, including *Becoming: What Makes a Woman*, published by University of Nebraska Gender Programs, and *Every River On Earth: Writing from Appalachian Ohio*, published by Ohio University Press. Moore is an Associate Professor of English and the Writing Center Director at Taylor University, where she is the poetry editor of *Relief Journal*. You can learn more about her work at julielmoore.com.

Cameron Morse Morse lives with his wife Lili and two children in Independence, Missouri. His poems have been published in numerous magazines, including *New Letters*, *Bridge Eight*, *Portland Review* and *South Dakota Review*. His first collection, *Fall Risk*, won Glass Lyre Press's 2018 Best Book Award. His latest is *Baldy* (Spartan Press, 2020). He holds an MFA from the University of Kansas City—Missouri and serves as Senior Reviews editor at *Harbor Review* and Poetry editor at *Harbor Editions*. For more information, check out his Facebook page or website.

Thomas Osatchoff, together with family, is building a self-sustaining home near a waterfall in The Philippines. Recent work has appeared in *Adjacent Pineapple*, *Barzakh Magazine*, *In Parentheses*, and elsewhere.

Lynn Pattison lives in Kalamazoo, Michigan. Her work has appeared in *Ruminate*, *Moon City Review*, *The Mom Egg Review*, *Glassworks Magazine* and *Notre Dame Review*, among others, and has been anthologized widely. Her published collections include the book, *Light That Sounds Like Breaking* (Mayapple Press), and three chapbooks: *tesla's daughter* (March St. Press), *Walking Back the Cat* (Bright Hill Press), and *Matryoshka Houses*, released last summer from Kelsay Press. Her book mss, *Milky Way Stardust Aquarium* is in search of a loving home.

Akshaya Pawaskar is a doctor practicing in India and poetry is her passion. Her poems have been published in *Tipton Poetry Journal*, *the punch magazine*, *Shards*, *The Blue Nib*, *North of Oxford*, *Indian Ruminations*, *Rock & Sling* among many others. She had been chosen as the winner of ekphrastic poetry competition 2020 by Craven arts council, third place winner of Poetry Matters Project contest 2020 and second place winner of *The Blue Nib* chapbook contest 2018.

Nancy Kay Peterson's poetry has appeared in print and online in numerous publications, including most recently *Lost Lake Folk Opera*, *One Sentence Poems*, *Spank the Carp* and *Three Line Poetry*. From 2004-2009, she was co-publisher and co-editor of *Main Channel Voices: A Dam Fine Literary Magazine*. Her chapbook, *Belated Remembrance*, was published by Finishing Line Press in 2010. A second chapbook, *Selling the Family*, is due out soon. She lives in Winona, Minnesota.

Timothy Robbins has been teaching English as a Second Language for 30 years. His poems have appeared in many literary journals and has published five volumes of poetry: *Three New Poets* (Hanging Loose Press), *Denny's Arbor Vitae* (Adelaide Books), *Carrying Bodies* (Main Street Rag Press) *Mother Wheel* (Cholla Needles Press) and *This Night I Sup in Your House* (Cyberwit.net). He lives in Wisconsin with his husband of 22 years.

Seth Rosenbloom grew up outside Washington D.C. and lives in Seattle. He studied acting at Boston University and received a BA in Drama from the University of Washington. Alongside a career in management consulting, he has written and acted in solo performances at On the Boards, Bumbershoot and on the Seattle Channel. He studies poetry at Hugo House, and is working on a collection of poems about coming of age and loss.

65

Michael Salcman: poet, physician and art historian, was chairman of neurosurgery at the University of Maryland and president of the Contemporary Museum. Poems appear in *Arts & Letters, The Café Review, Hopkins Review, The Hudson Review, New Letters,* and *Poet Lore*. Books include *The Clock Made of Confetti, The Enemy of Good is Better, Poetry in Medicine*, his popular anthology of classic and contemporary poems on doctors, patients, illness & healing, *A Prague Spring, Before & After*, winner of the 2015 Sinclair Poetry Prize, and *Shades & Graces*, inaugural winner of The Daniel Hoffman Legacy Book Prize (Spuyten Duyvil, 2020). He lives in Baltimore.

Hamilton Salsich is a teacher, husband, and father of four who lives in Connecticut and has been published in a number of journals, most recently *Common Ground Review, White Pelican Review, Fox Cry Review, The Paper Street Journal, Amarolla, Briar Cliff Review,* and *Tiny Seed Literary Journal*.

Sara Sarna is a poet in southeastern Wisconsin. She is a military "brat" and only put down roots as an adult. Her work has appeared in print, online and on stage. Her first chapbook, *Whispers from a Bench*, was published in November of 2020.

Leslie Schultz (Northfield, Minnesota) is the author of three collections of poetry, *Still Life with Poppies: Elegies* (Kelsay Books, 2016), *Cloud Song* (Kelsay Books, 2018)., and *Concertina* (Kelsay Books, 2019) Her poetry has appeared most recently in *Poet Lore, North Dakota Quarterly, Able Muse, Blue Unicorn Journal, Light, Mezzo Cammin, Swamp Lily Review, Third Wednesday, The Madison Review, The Midwest Quarterly, The Orchards Poetry Journal,* and *The Wayfarer*; in the sidewalks of Northfield; and in a chapbook, *Living Room* (Midwestern Writers' Publishing House). She received a Pushcart Prize nomination in 2017 and has had three winning poems in the Maria W. Faust sonnet contest (2013, 2016, 2019). Schultz posts poems, photographs, and essays on her website: www.winonamedia.net.

Dave Seter is the author of *Don't Sing to Me of Electric Fences*, due out from Cherry Grove Collections in 2021. His poems and critical works have appeared in *Paterson Literary Review, The Hopper, Raven Chronicles, Palaver, Confluence,* and other journals. He has received two Pushcart nominations. He is currently on the Board of Directors of the Marin Poetry Center. He earned his undergraduate degree in civil engineering from Princeton University and his graduate degree in humanities from Dominican University of California. Born in Chicago, he now lives in Sonoma County, California.

Mary Shanley is a poet/writer who lives in New York City. Her poetry is informed by the spiritual nature of life, the mysteries of life, the landscape of New York City and beyond. Four of her books have been published: *Hobo Code Poems* by Vox Pop Press; *Things They Left Behind, Poems for Faces* and *Mott Street Stories* and *Las Vegas Stories* by Side Street Press. Mary publishes online at: *Blaze Vox, Dream Noir, Underground Voices, Mobius, Radius, Mr. Bellers's Neighborhood, Blue Lake Review, Logos Journal, Hobo Camp Review, StepAway Magazine, Anak Sastra Journal, Shangra-la Magazine* and more. She was the Featured Poet on WBAI fmRadio NYC, and was nominated for a Pushcart Prize.

Raj Sharma lives in North Carolina and is a retired senior professor of English who has worked at universities in India, Middle East and USA. Published work includes two collections of short stories, *A Strange Wind Blowing* (2019) and *In My Arms* (2000) and a collection of poems, *No Season for Grief* (2017). Over forty poems and short stories have appeared in magazines like *Grey Sparrow, North Dakota Quarterly, Crossways, The American Aesthetic, SNReview. South Jersey Underground, The Monarch Review, Folly, JD Review, The Fine Line, TWJ Magazine, The Missing Slate, Exercise Bowler, Rock and Sling, Ascent Aspirations, Dr TJ Eckleburg Review, New Mercury Magazine* and others.

Michael E. Strosahl is a midwestern river-born poet, originally from Moline, Illinois, now living in Jefferson City, Missouri. Besides several appearances in the *Tipton Poetry Journal*, Maik's work has appeared in *Flying Island, Bards Against Hunger* projects, on buses, in museums and online at *indianavoicejournal, poetrysuperhighway* and *projectagentorange*. Maik also has a weekly poetry column at the online blog *Moristotle & Company*.

James Eric Watkins has dramatically performed his poetry at the Madison-Jefferson County (Indiana) Public Library, the University of Southern Indiana, and at Indiana University Southeast, as well as at the Village Lights Bookstore in Madison, Indiana and other venues. James' creative work has appeared in *Acorn, The Scioto Voice Newspaper, The Main Street Rag, Pegasus, Tipton Poetry Journal, Visions, Moments of the Soul* and many others.

Diane Webster's goal is to remain open to poetry ideas in everyday life, nature or an overheard phrase and to write. Diane, who lives in Colorado, enjoys the challenge of transforming images into words to fit her poems. Her work has appeared in *Philadelphia Poets, Old Red Kimono, Home Planet News Online* and other literary magazines.

Made in the USA
Columbia, SC
07 March 2021